FAITH
Foundations

A STUDY ON THE BASICS OF CHRISTIANITY

AUBREY COLEMAN

Study Suggestions

We believe that the Bible is true, trustworthy, and timeless and that it is vitally important for all believers. These study suggestions are intended to help you more effectively study Scripture as you seek to know and love God through His Word.

SUGGESTED STUDY TOOLS

- A Bible

- A double-spaced, printed copy of the Scripture passages that this study covers. You can use a website like *www.biblegateway.com* to copy the text of a passage and print out a double-spaced copy to be able to mark on easily

- A journal to write notes or prayers

- Pens, colored pencils, and highlighters

- A dictionary to look up unfamiliar words

HOW TO USE THIS STUDY

Begin your study time in prayer. Ask God to reveal Himself to you, to help you understand what you are reading, and to transform you with His Word (Psalm 119:18).

Before you read what is written in each day of the study itself, read the assigned passages of Scripture for that day. Use your double-spaced copy to circle, underline, highlight, draw arrows, and mark in any way you would like to help you dig deeper as you work through a passage.

Read the daily written content provided for the current study day.

Answer the questions that appear at the end of each study day.

HOW TO STUDY THE BIBLE

The inductive method provides tools for deeper and more intentional Bible study. To study the Bible inductively, work through the steps below after reading background information on the book.

1 OBSERVATION & COMPREHENSION
Key question: What does the text say?

After reading the daily Scripture in its entirety at least once, begin working with smaller portions of the Scripture. Read a passage of Scripture repetitively, and then mark the following items in the text:

- Key or repeated words and ideas
- Key themes
- Transition words (Ex: therefore, but, because, if/then, likewise, etc.)
- Lists
- Comparisons and contrasts
- Commands
- Unfamiliar words (look these up in a dictionary)
- Questions you have about the text

2 INTERPRETATION
Key question: What does the text mean?

Once you have annotated the text, work through the following steps to help you interpret its meaning:

- Read the passage in other versions for a better understanding of the text.
- Read cross-references to help interpret Scripture with Scripture.
- Paraphrase or summarize the passage to check for understanding.
- Identify how the text reflects the metanarrative of Scripture, which is the story of creation, fall, redemption, and restoration.
- Read trustworthy commentaries if you need further insight into the meaning of the passage.

3 APPLICATION
Key Question: How should the truth of this passage change me?

Bible study is not merely an intellectual pursuit. The truths about God, ourselves, and the gospel that we discover in Scripture should produce transformation in our hearts and lives. Answer the following questions as you consider what you have learned in your study:

- What attributes of God's character are revealed in the passage?

    Consider places where the text directly states the character of God, as well as how His character is revealed through His words and actions.

- What do I learn about myself in light of who God is?

    Consider how you fall short of God's character, how the text reveals your sin nature, and what it says about your new identity in Christ.

- How should this truth change me?

    A passage of Scripture may contain direct commands telling us what to do or warnings about sins to avoid in order to help us grow in holiness. Other times our application flows out of seeing ourselves in light of God's character. As we pray and reflect on how God is calling us to change in light of His Word, we should be asking questions like, "How should I pray for God to change my heart?" and "What practical steps can I take toward cultivating habits of holiness?"

THE ATTRIBUTES OF GOD

ETERNAL
God has no beginning and no end. He always was, always is, and always will be.

HAB. 1:12 / REV. 1:8 / IS. 41:4

FAITHFUL
God is incapable of anything but fidelity. He is loyally devoted to His plan and purpose.

2 TIM. 2:13 / DEUT. 7:9
HEB. 10:23

GOOD
God is pure; there is no defilement in Him. He is unable to sin, and all He does is good.

GEN. 1:31 / PS. 34:8 / PS. 107:1

GRACIOUS
God is kind, giving us gifts and benefits we do not deserve.

2 KINGS 13:23 / PS. 145:8
IS. 30:18

HOLY
God is undefiled and unable to be in the presence of defilement. He is sacred and set-apart.

REV. 4:8 / LEV. 19:2 / HAB. 1:13

INCOMPREHENSIBLE & TRANSCENDENT
God is high above and beyond human understanding. He is unable to be fully known.

PS. 145:3 / IS. 55:8-9
ROM. 11:33-36

IMMUTABLE
God does not change. He is the same yesterday, today, and tomorrow.

1 SAM. 15:29 / ROM. 11:29
JAMES 1:17

INFINITE
God is limitless. He exhibits all of His attributes perfectly and boundlessly.

ROM. 11:33-36 / IS. 40:28
PS. 147:5

JEALOUS
God is desirous of receiving the praise and affection He rightly deserves.

EX. 20:5 / DEUT. 4:23-24
JOSH. 24:19

JUST
God governs in perfect justice. He acts in accordance with justice. In Him, there is no wrongdoing or dishonesty.

IS. 61:8 / DEUT. 32:4 / PS. 146:7-9

LOVING
God is eternally, enduringly, steadfastly loving and affectionate. He does not forsake or betray His covenant love.

JN. 3:16 / EPH. 2:4-5 / 1 JN. 4:16

MERCIFUL
God is compassionate, withholding from us the wrath that we deserve.

TITUS 3:5 / PS. 25:10
LAM. 3:22-23

OMNIPOTENT
God is all-powerful; His strength is unlimited.

MAT. 19:26 / JOB 42:1-2
JER. 32:27

OMNIPRESENT
God is everywhere; His presence is near and permeating.

PROV. 15:3 / PS. 139:7-10
JER. 23:23-24

OMNISCIENT
God is all-knowing; there is nothing unknown to Him.

PS. 147:4 / I JN. 3:20
HEB. 4:13

PATIENT
God is long-suffering and enduring. He gives ample opportunity for people to turn toward Him.

ROM. 2:4 / 2 PET. 3:9 / PS. 86:15

SELF-EXISTENT
God was not created but exists by His power alone.

PS. 90:1-2 / JN. 1:4 / JN. 5:26

SELF-SUFFICIENT
God has no needs and depends on nothing, but everything depends on God.

IS. 40:28-31 / ACTS 17:24-25
PHIL. 4:19

SOVEREIGN
God governs over all things; He is in complete control.

COL. 1:17 / PS. 24:1-2
1 CHRON. 29:11-12

TRUTHFUL
God is our measurement of what is fact. By Him we are able to discern true and false.

JN. 3:33 / ROM. 1:25 / JN. 14:6

WISE
God is infinitely knowledgeable and is judicious with His knowledge.

IS. 46:9-10 / IS. 55:9 / PROV. 3:19

WRATHFUL
God stands in opposition to all that is evil. He enacts judgment according to His holiness, righteousness, and justice.

PS. 69:24 / JN. 3:36 / ROM. 1:18

Study Suggestions

METANARRATIVE OF SCRIPTURE

Creation

In the beginning, God created the universe. He made the world and everything in it. He created humans in His own image to be His representatives on the earth.

Fall

The first humans, Adam and Eve, disobeyed God by eating from the fruit of the Tree of Knowledge of Good and Evil. Their disobedience impacted the whole world. The punishment for sin is death, and because of Adam's original sin, all humans are sinful and condemned to death.

Redemption

God sent His Son to become a human and redeem His people. Jesus Christ lived a sinless life but died on the cross to pay the penalty for sin. He resurrected from the dead and ascended into heaven. All who put their faith in Jesus are saved from death and freely receive the gift of eternal life.

Restoration

One day, Jesus Christ will return again and restore all that sin destroyed. He will usher in a new heaven and new earth where all who trust in Him will live eternally with glorified bodies in the presence of God.

in this study

Introduction 10

week 1

The Bible 13
Who is God? 17
The Beginning 21
What is Sin? 25
The Promised Sacrifice 29
Scripture Memory 32
Weekly Reflection 34

week 2

Jesus Christ, the Son of God 37
+ C.S. Lewis: Liar, Lunatic, or Lord 40
There is Only One Way to Be Saved 43
A New Identity 47
The Holy Spirit 51
What Happens in the End? 55
Scripture Memory 58
Weekly Reflection 60

week 3

Studying the Bible 63
+ Helpful Ways to Begin Studying the Bible 66
Prayer 71
Evangelism and Fellowship 75
The Church 79
Reflect and Respond 83
Scripture Memory 86
Weekly Reflection 88
+ Suggested Next Steps 90

introduction

The idea of better understanding the Christian faith may evoke a number of thoughts and feelings. Maybe Christianity confuses you and leaves you searching for answers. Maybe you recently heard the gospel of Jesus Christ for the first time, and you are hoping to hear more of what this good news means for your life. Maybe you are hurt and angry because of your personal experiences associated with Christianity. Maybe you are apprehensive and afraid of how your life could change after knowing more. You might even find yourself in a distant place, longing to remember the truths of the gospel and how that can shape your faith. No matter where you find yourself—curious, confused, distant, or hopeful—you are in the right place.

The heart behind this study is to provide a basic foundation for understanding the Christian faith by answering questions like:
Why trust the Bible? Who is God? What is sin? Why do I need salvation? Why is Jesus different from every other religious leader? What does the Bible say about life after death?

To prepare, take a moment to list out your thoughts, feelings, apprehensions, and questions as you begin this study.

week 1 - day 1

"

We grow to know and understand God because of the Bible.

The Bible

READ ISAIAH 40:8, 2 TIMOTHY 3:16–17, HEBREWS 4:12

We all operate out of a certain worldview—a set of beliefs that directs and points us to what is true. For the Christian, the foundation for everything we believe begins with the belief that God existed before the foundation of the world. He is the Creator of all things, and He has revealed Himself to His creation through the Bible. Therefore, we cling to His Word for truth because we can trust God is who He says He is. We understand that the Bible is good and true because it is inspired by God, and the original manuscripts were without error.

The Bible holds 66 books, was written by 40 authors in multiple languages, and took more than 1,500 years to complete. It is divided into an Old Testament and a New Testament. Though the Old Testament includes the word "old" in its name, it certainly is not irrelevant or outdated. Instead, the Old Testament is the first half of the Bible, and it records the creation of the world and God's relationship with His people before Jesus Christ was born. The New Testament records the life and ministry of Jesus, everything that came after His death, and what to expect in the end times.

Due to its varying authorship, genres, languages, and styles, some may question the Bible's validity or wonder why we should believe what it says. We must begin by answering this question with 2 Timothy 3:16, which says, "All Scripture is inspired by God and is profitable for teaching, for rebuking, for correcting, for training in righteousness." This means that all of Scripture came from the same source, God.

To say the Word of God is inspired, in biblical terms means, "breathed out" by God. The Apostle Peter explains this in 2 Peter 1:20–21, "Above all, you know this: No prophecy of Scripture comes from the prophet's own interpretation, because no prophecy ever came by the will of man; instead, men spoke from God as they were carried along by the Holy Spirit." God's Word was inspired, or breathed out, for godly men to record and for Christians to read and follow. Therefore, God is the definitive and true author. He is the author of the very words we see written on the pages by the hands of those He inspired to write them.

Even though the Bible was physically written by men, we can trust that the original manuscripts were written without any error. Regardless of life experience, personality, writing style, grammar, vocabulary, or penmanship, God used people to communicate His message in precisely the way He wanted it to be communicated. In fact, God's Word is incapable of error. God is holy in all He says and does, and He will accomplish all that He wants to through His written Word (Isaiah 55:11).

Everything that we believe about God and the Bible must go hand in hand. We grow to know and understand God because of the Bible, and the Bible gives credence to who God says He is and how it impacts our understanding of His Word. Hebrews 6:18 says it is impossible for God to lie. Because God is the author, incapable of lying, we must trust that His Word is incapable of error. The Bible cannot be anything but true.

The Bible is essential to the Christian faith. God communicates His plan, His purposes, and His intentions to the world through its very pages. This does not mean all of our questions will be answered by Scripture, but it does mean that everything we need to know in order to live faithfully as Christians is recorded in the books of the Bible. Scripture serves as a tangible tool for us to interpret and understand the world we live in, it connects the gospel of Jesus Christ to our everyday lives, and it serves as the means by which we grow in our understanding and knowledge of God.

"Everything we need to know in order to live faithfully as Christians is recorded in the books of the Bible."

Take a moment to consider what shapes your worldview. How have those things determined the way you live?

What is your understanding of the Bible?

How does your understanding of the Bible shape the way you think about God?

week 1 - day 2

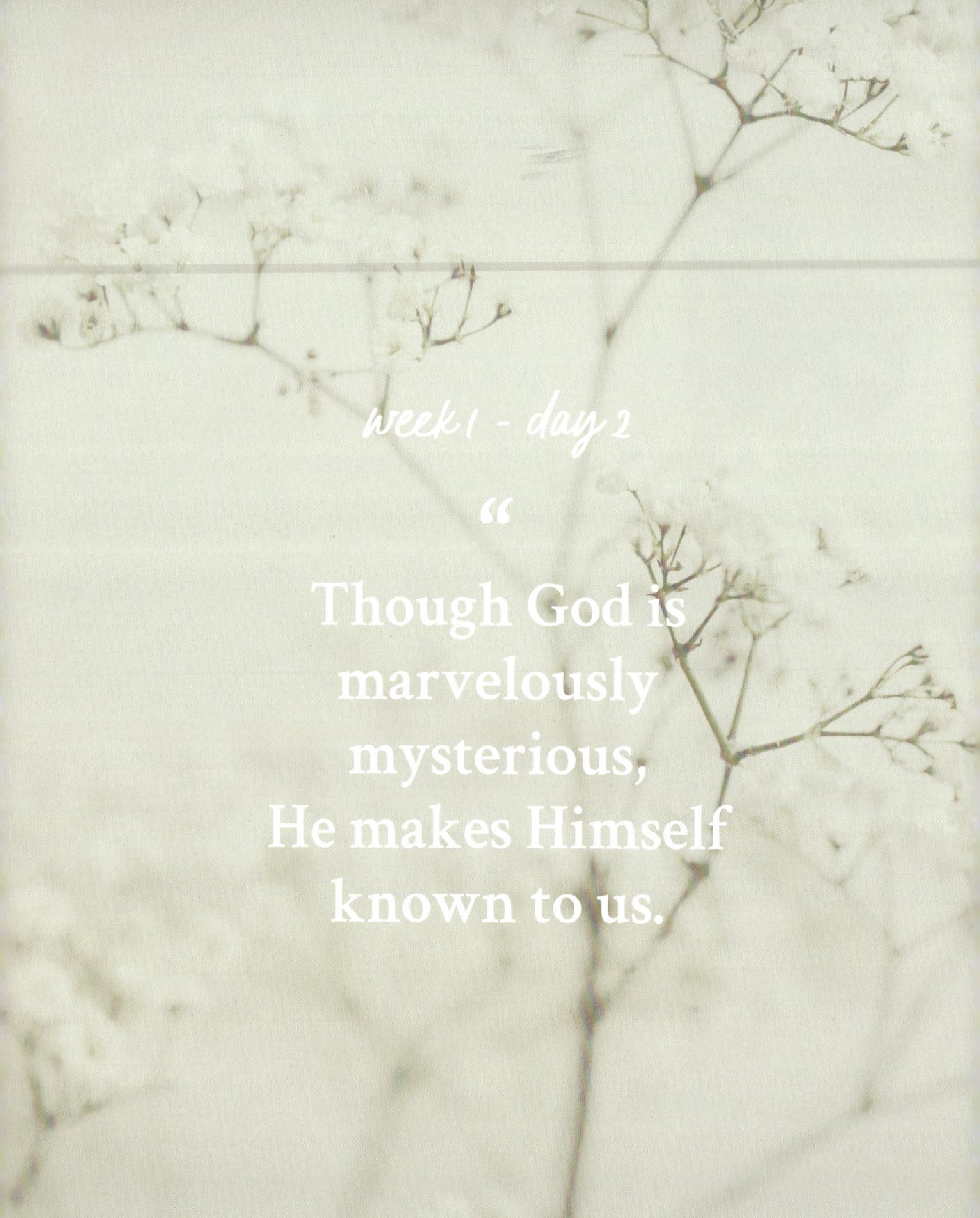

"

Though God is marvelously mysterious, He makes Himself known to us.

Who is God?

READ GENESIS 1:1, NUMBERS 23:19, 1 CORINTHIANS 8:6

Everything we seek to understand about the world hinges on how we answer this question: who is God? Who we understand Him to be determines how we view everything else. As you enter into this study, you likely hold some kind of view of who God is. If you see God as a type of Santa Claus, you likely expect your relationship with Him to be determined by your behavior, whether you are good or bad. If you see God as a distant dictator pointing His finger and making commands, you likely misunderstand His compassion and His deep love for His people. If you try to fit God into a box of what intellectually makes the most sense to you, you will undoubtedly limit your understanding of Him.

Maybe you think of Him in some other way. But because the Bible is inspired by God, it is the best and most necessary place for us to ask questions about who He really is. In the opening sentences of the first book of the Bible, Genesis, it is written, "In the beginning God created the heavens and the earth." Before the world and anything came to be, God existed. Nobody made God. He just is, always has been, and always will be (Revelation 1:8). He is the beginning of all things, and all things were made and are sustained by Him.

God created everything—light, oxygen, cells, water, plants of every kind, a diverse array of animals, and everything with form and purpose. Then, He created man and woman differently than everything else. In the beginning, everything and everyone was created by God, and He called His creation good. Every part of creation was meant to display the wonders and glories of God. Romans 1:20 explains that "[God's] invisible attributes, that is, his eternal power and divine nature, have been clearly seen since the creation of the world, being understood through what he has made." Humanity is without excuse since God clearly makes Himself known to us through all of creation and through His Word.

God is not like us; He is Spirit. John 4:24 says, "God is spirit, and those who worship him must worship in Spirit and in truth." He is not confined to a body or the conditions of this world. He is not limited by space and time in the way that we are. He can be everywhere at any time. He is invisible and unseen. Yet He sees all and knows all. His understanding and knowledge are so vast and so wide, it is beyond what we could ever conjure up in our own minds. God is not like anything we have ever known. He is higher than every aspect of His creation in every possible way.

God is also three persons: Father, Son, and Holy Spirit. Another way of phrasing this aspect of God is that He is Trinity. This does not mean that God is three gods, but rather, He is three persons in one God. They are distinct and yet united in nature. They do not exist apart from one another, and they share the same exact nature. This can be a challenging concept for many, and truthfully, there will be many things about God that we find mysterious and beyond our limited understanding. But what a Trinitarian God communicates to us is that He is relational. This means that God the Father, God the Son, and God the Spirit dwell together in harmony, united by love and holiness.

Another aspect of God's character is that He is holy. The word "holy" as biblically defined means "sacred, set apart." This word is only applicable to God because He is sacred and set apart from every other created thing. There is no one holy like the Lord, and there is no one like Him (1 Samuel 2:2). The holiness of God is one of His most profound attributes. A. W. Tozer, in his book, *The Knowledge of the Holy*, wrote this about God's holiness: "Holy is the way God is. To be holy He does not conform to a standard. He is that standard. He is holy with an infinite, incomprehensible fullness of purity that is incapable of being other than it is." Not only is God holy in His actions, but He is also holy in His essence. All that He is and does is holy.

God rules supreme over the heavens and the earth and holds sovereign authority over all. He is above all things and before all things (John 3:31, Colossians 1:15–20). Everything exists within His plan and purposes. He knows everything completely before it comes to be (Romans 11:33–34). He can do and accomplish anything He pleases at any time and in any way. Nothing is impossible for Him (Jeremiah 32:17). Nothing happens outside of His knowledge and will. He holds power and authority over all things in heaven and earth.

The intricacies of the nature and character of God are inexhaustible. We can spend our entire lives learning about Him and knowing more. Even in light of His power, holiness, and supreme attributes, we are remiss if we do not know this truth about Him—He deeply loves and desires a relationship with His people. We can easily learn about Him and assume He is distant. We can assume He is uninvolved in His creation, directing and guiding from afar. Though God is grand, He desires to draw near. And though God is marvelously mysterious, He makes Himself known to us. The story of the Bible is the story of God pursuing His people in love, and He would stop at nothing to make a way to have a relationship with them again.

"The story of the Bible is the story of God pursuing His people in love."

What is your understanding of God? How do you view your relationship with God?

What characteristic of God stands out most to you and why?

What did you read today that challenged or encouraged your view of God?

week 1 - day 3

"

Though sin destroys our relationship with God, Jesus Christ came to the world to restore what was broken.

The Beginning

READ GENESIS 1–3

When we look around today, we are surrounded by life and detail. Where did it all begin? Some may suggest that all that exists in the world came to be by a collision of particles and atoms. But when we look around to see the color of the leaves in the fall, the rhythm of the ocean, the majesty of the mountains, the birds making songs in the morning, and of course, the unique wonder of humanity, it only makes sense that the world was created. Atoms and particles could never self-create with such purpose, order, and beauty. Life was born from something, rather Someone, much greater, more powerful, and more intentional. The Bible tells us that the Creator of the world is God.

The book of Genesis gives us a glimpse into how everything we see now came to be. When God created the world, He began with light. Then He made the sky, land and water, fruits and vegetation. He created the sun and the moon and the stars. He created land animals, sea creatures, and birds of the air. But He saved His most treasured creation for last: mankind. God created man and woman in His image, meaning we possess His nature like no other form of creation. We have the ability to feel as He feels, to understand, and to know Him more in our likeness.

When God made man and all of creation, He said it was very good (Genesis 1:31). Every part of creation was perfect and without flaws. In His infinite wisdom and understanding, God knew all His people needed to live and thrive, and He created exactly that. The first man, named Adam, and the first woman, named Eve, lived in a perfect and harmonious relationship with God. They lived in a place called the garden of Eden, where everything they ever needed was there. Their role in all creation was to enjoy a relationship with God, cultivate the land, and multiply their family.

Everything God created, every detail and component of His creation, was intended to glorify Him and serve His people. The one command given to the man and woman was not to eat the fruit of a specific tree in the garden, the Tree of

Knowledge of Good and Evil. And the reasoning? Because if they ate from it, they would surely die (Genesis 2:16–17). In most cases, that would be a good enough reason to stay away from this tree. Not to mention, Adam and Eve lived in paradise, unashamed, in a harmonious relationship with God, and they were provided for in every way.

Adam and Eve eventually encountered a serpent in Genesis 3, which God called the most cunning animal of His creation. This serpent was an instrument of Satan, and he tempted Eve with a challenge to God's command to not eat of the Tree of Knowledge of Good and Evil. The serpent asked, "Did God really say, 'You can't eat from any tree in the garden'?" (Genesis 3:1). Eve reiterated God's command, but the serpent argued, "No! You will certainly not die… In fact, God knows that when you eat it your eyes will be opened and you will be like God, knowing good and evil" (Genesis 3:4–5). The serpent was encouraging the first humans not only to question their Creator but to disobey His command. Unfortunately, Adam and Eve chose to eat from the forbidden tree, and the consequences would bring a ripple effect of disobedience for every generation that followed. From that point on, sin was woven into the heart of humanity, and there was no longer blissful innocence. All of the world would bear the effects of sin, longing for the restoration and redemption only their Maker and Creator could provide.

God created us to worship Him. We worship through obedience to His commands and through loving Him with our whole hearts. But because of our sin, we stray from worshiping God and worship other things we think will satisfy our needs—wealth, love, success, and the list goes on. But only God can fill the void in our hearts. Our hearts were crafted to find fulfillment in Him. Our lives were given to us to find purpose in Him. And we find true security in our relationship with Him. Though sin destroys our relationship with God, Jesus Christ came to the world to restore what was broken. Through salvation in Him, God gives us new hearts to find our complete and total fulfillment in Him.

Who could know us better than the One who formed us from the inside out? Who could care for us better than the One who knows our every thought and intention? Who could love us more than the One who dreamt of us before the foundations of the world? There is no other who is truly worthy of all of our worship and obedience—only our Creator, the God of the Bible.

"Only God can fill the void in our hearts."

What is your understanding or belief about how the world began?

How does your understanding of God shape those beliefs?

How does the Bible shape the way you view creation and the world?

week 1 - day 4

"
God had a redemptive plan from the very beginning.

What is Sin?

READ ROMANS 3:23, ROMANS 6:23, JAMES 1:14–15

If asked, "Are you a good person?" What might you say? Some of us might think about who, from the world's perspective, are some of the worst people to have ever lived on this earth—Adolph Hitler, Joseph Stalin, Saddam Hussein, or Ivan the Terrible. Compared to them, we would say we are doing great! We may even think about the murderers, abusers, and thieves of the world and consider ourselves much more morally upright. But the truth is that anyone who falls short of God's standard of righteousness is not good. And Romans 3:10 says, "As it is written: There is no one righteous, not even one."

The topic of sin can feel harsh and challenging, but understanding sin is crucial to our understanding of humanity and our broken relationship with God. The term "sin" originates from the Old English word "synn," which is translated from biblical Greek to portray the action of missing the mark, often in terms of spear throwing. Applying the definition to Christianity, sin is missing the mark of obedience to God's law and commands. We either perfectly obey, or we do not. And those who fall short of God's righteous requirements are sinners.

Because God is holy, He requires perfect obedience to be in a right relationship with Him. He cannot be in the presence of sin. Therefore, when Adam and Eve first sinned and disobeyed God's command, God cast them out of His presence and out of the garden. Their sin broke the loving and harmonious relationship they previously shared with Him.

When sin entered the world, it brought about rebellion. What was once a world full of order became disordered and chaotic. All of creation was infiltrated with the knowledge of evil, and the wickedness of humanity grew and grew. The first half of Romans 6:23 says, "For the wages of sin is death…" Our sin is deserving of death. When God commanded Adam and Eve not to eat from the tree, He told them they would surely die if they disobeyed.

There are three types of death mentioned in the Bible. Physical death is when the body dies. Spiritual death is separation from a relationship with God. And eternal death is a permanent separation from God forever. Adam and Eve experienced a spiritual death as a result of their sin. They were separated from God's presence. They also were promised a physical death when the Lord said, "you will return to dust" (Genesis 3:19). God could have struck them down in a moment. But the fact that He let them live reveals His gracious character. Even more so, we will see that God, in His all-inclusive knowledge, knew what Adam and Eve would do, and God had a plan to save His people from their sin all along.

Because of our sin, we, too, are separated from a relationship with God. You may wonder how the sin of two people could determine the wickedness of every generation that followed. Romans 5:12 tell us, "sin entered the world through one man, and death through sin, in this way death spread to all people, because all sinned." We inherited the curse of sin through Adam, and we, too, choose rebellion. We respond to God just like Adam and Eve. We choose our own way, and we reject His commands.

We often indulge in some of the things the world tells us will make us happy—wealth, lust, love, power, successes, fame, or possessions—even at the cost of rejecting the only One who can truly satisfy our every need: God. We may be tempted to think of ourselves too highly, but consider your morality. Have you ever lied? Have you ever been greedy? Have you ever been unkind? Have you ever hated someone? Have you ever gossiped? We have all sinned. Even if we cannot name it in our actions, we can certainly see sin evident in our hearts. We are imperfect people, and we fall short of God's standards every single day. Though we all struggle in our own way, because we are quick to worship ourselves and our own interests over His, we are all guilty before a holy God.

But how do we know what God requires for our obedience? The Bible reveals God's standard of righteousness for humanity. We see it plainly displayed in the Old Testament when Moses presented the Ten Commandments in Exodus 20. We see it again, further expounded on in the New Testament when Jesus gave His Sermon on the Mount in Matthew 5–7. But even without ever reading the Law, it is written in our hearts (Romans 2:15). In the book of Romans, Paul explained that although the Law was not given to the Gentiles (those who were not Jewish), everyone still has the innate knowledge and understanding to distinguish between good and evil. Because man was created in the image of God, we all have a God-given ability to know right and wrong. Our consciences will bear witness to what we believe in our hearts, and our actions will indicate whether we obey or not.

In light of understanding our sinful nature, it is important to note that God does not desire sheer morality; He desires people who love and worship Him. So what can be done when people are sinful? What can change the course of generations of people continuing to sin? Fortunately, the failure of humanity is not the end of the story for God's people. God had a redemptive plan from the very beginning. He knew the disorder man would cause, and He prepared a way for a Savior to restore what was broken. He brought a shining promise of hope in Genesis 3:15—that He would send a Savior to crush the deceptive serpent and defeat sin and death once and for all. He would make a way to pay for the sins of His people and clothe them with righteousness through the gift of His very own Son, Jesus Christ.

What is your standard for morality, or what represents your moral compass?

How does your understanding of sin shape the way you view the world?

What is God's standard for righteousness, and how do you measure up? How will you meet the mark?

week 1 - day 5

"

The gospel is God's way of saving sinners through the life, death, and resurrection of Jesus Christ.

The Promised Sacrifice

READ GENESIS 3:15, ISAIAH 9:6, JOHN 3:16

In the Old Testament, sins were paid for by making atonement. Atonement involved animal sacrifice, and by the innocent animal's bloodshed, God would see the sins of the person who offered the sacrifice as paid for or covered. God commanded this sacrifice as a means to be in a relationship with His people. Those who desired to know God would offer sacrifices for the sin that kept them from a relationship with Him. However, those who did not make sacrifices for their sin were spiritually separated from God, unable to commune with Him.

In Genesis 3, when Adam and Eve first sinned, they hid because they were ashamed of their disobedience to God. In response, God graciously gave an example of the first animal sacrifice by clothing them with animal skins and covering their sin (Genesis 3:21). These sacrifices continued throughout the Old Testament as a way for people to fellowship with God.

However, God never intended for this sacrificial system to be the ultimate answer for resolving the sins of His people. Rather, it was meant to point all people to the One who would come to offer His own life in order to pay for our sins once and for all. The blood of an animal could never remove sin completely because there would always need to be another sacrifice. As Hebrews 10:4 confirms, "For it is impossible for the blood of bulls and goats to take away sins." Rather, animal sacrifices served as a temporary covering.

The truth is, our sin has to be paid for. Our sin disrupts God's holy order. It brings death and darkness and serves as a selfish response to God's love and grace toward His people. Our sin is a rejection of God, and He will unleash His holy wrath on all who exalt evil and sin with their lives.

You may wonder what that really means. Well, for anyone who remains in sin, whose sin is not paid for, they will not only be spiritually separated from God in this lifetime and eternally separated from God after death. They will also experience the weight of God's wrath—His holy retribution and justice—when they stand before His throne at the end of their lives. Every person on this planet will stand before God and give an account of themselves (Romans 14:12). And every single sin will bear the consequences of God's wrath. The distinction for Christians is that instead of standing before God's throne with sin that has yet to be paid for, we stand with sin that is covered by the sacrifice of Jesus Christ on the cross.

God knew the death and destruction sin would bring. So He sent His one and only Son, Jesus Christ, to pay the penalty for our sins, so we could have a restored relationship with Him. Not only has Christ paid the penalty for sin, but He will return to defeat sin once and for all. His victorious defeat over Satan is foretold in the opening chapters of the Bible. In Genesis 3:15, God tells the serpent, "I will put hostility between you and the woman, and between your offspring and her offspring. He will strike your head, and you will strike his heel."

According to this verse, after the serpent deceived Eve, God told the serpent He would place hostility between the serpent and Eve—a blood feud between their offspring. Generations and generations came and went, and eventually, the promised Savior was born from the seed of Eve to the virgin Mary. The serpent would strike the heel of the woman's offspring—a promise that was fulfilled through the crucifixion of Christ on the cross. Jesus Christ died on our behalf, bearing the wrath of God for our willing disobedience so that we could be united with Him again. The phrase "strike his heel" suggests that Jesus's pain was not final. Though wounded for us, Jesus rose from the dead three days later, and God promises that Jesus Christ will deliver a fatal blow to Satan when He returns. With this, Jesus will strike the head of the serpent, just as promised in Genesis 3:15. Revelation 20 affirms God's promise of this defeat. When Christ returns, He will bind Satan up and throw him in the abyss (Revelation 20:1–3), eventually throwing him into the lake of fire as a final crushing act of declaring victory over him (Revelation 20:7–10).

The sacrificial blood of Jesus Christ shed on the cross can pay for and wash away the sins of anyone. This work is often referred to by Christians as the Gospel of Jesus Christ. The word "gospel" means "good news," and that is exactly what it is! The gospel is God's way of saving sinners through the life, death, and resurrection of Jesus Christ in order to restore their relationship with Him. Christ's sacrifice pays the penalty for past, present, and future sins for anyone who puts their hope and faith in Him. Through faith in Jesus, our sins are forgiven by God, and our relationship with Him is restored both now and forever. We are no longer spiritually dead, and though physical death is the reality of the world we live in, we will not experience eternal death, but our souls will live with God on into eternity.

Atonement in the Old Testament was a faith exercise. Today, through faith, we can humbly receive salvation through Jesus Christ and His sacrificial death on the cross. Jesus does more than temporarily pay for sin; He destroys it. And after He died, He rose from the grave so that He could defeat the power of sin and death once and for all for those who trust and believe in Him. Those who put their faith in Christ are fully forgiven by God. They will enjoy His presence now as they navigate life in this world, and they will enjoy His presence in full for eternity after.

What does the "atonement of sins" mean?

*Why were the Old Testament sacrifices only temporary?
What are the ways we try to temporarily deal with our sin?*

How was Jesus Christ's sacrifice different? Why was it necessary?

Week 1 Scripture Memory

FOR THE WAGES OF SIN IS DEATH,
BUT THE GIFT OF GOD IS ETERNAL LIFE
IN CHRIST JESUS OUR LORD.

ROMANS 6:23

Scripture Memory Practice

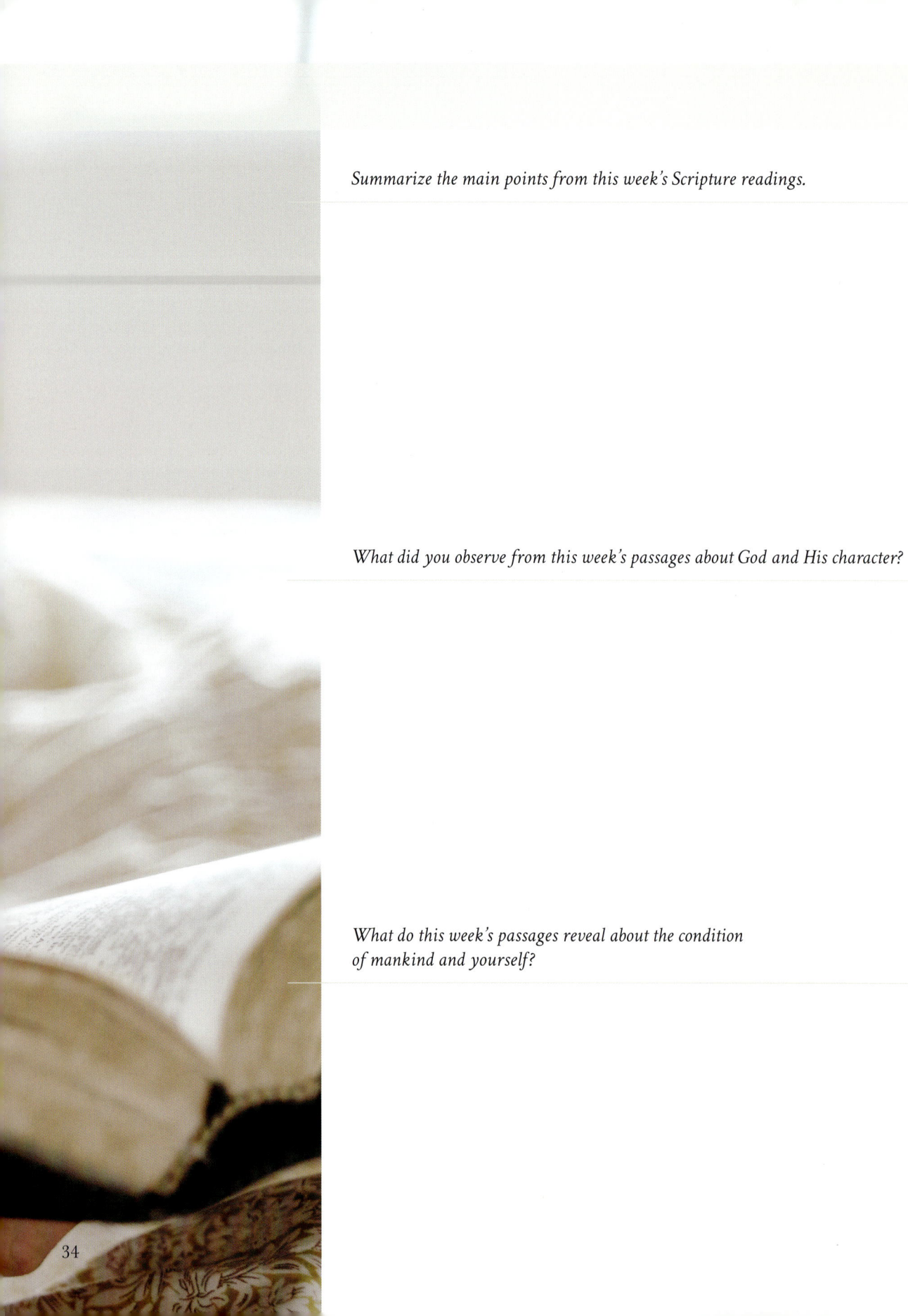

Summarize the main points from this week's Scripture readings.

What did you observe from this week's passages about God and His character?

What do this week's passages reveal about the condition of mankind and yourself?

Week 1 Reflection

REVIEW ALL PASSAGES FROM THE WEEK

How do these passages point to the gospel?

How should you respond to these Scriptures? What specific action steps can you take this week to apply them in your life?

Write a prayer in response to your study of God's Word. Adore God for who He is, confess sins that He revealed in your own life, ask Him to empower you to walk in obedience, and pray for anyone who comes to mind as you study.

week 2 - day 1

"

Our sin creates a chasm between God and us. But Jesus bridges the gap.

Jesus Christ, the Son of God

READ I TIMOTHY 2:5, JOHN 14:6, PHILIPPIANS 2:5–11

We have already mentioned Jesus Christ throughout this study. Maybe His name is familiar to you, or maybe you have never heard of Him until now. Historians and philosophers often highlight Jesus as a great moral teacher or a gifted religious leader. And though people may disagree on the details, many affirm that Jesus was an extraordinary man. But Jesus is much more than this—He is unlike any other figure in history. Why? Jesus Christ is the Son of God. Even if reading that statement gives you pause, you have to admit it is a claim worth exploring. So, let us jump in. Who is Jesus?

We get to know this man who lived thousands of years ago in a book more detailed than any other, the Bible. There we find detailed and personal eyewitness accounts of His life and teachings. The Gospels—which include the books of Matthew, Mark, Luke, and John in the New Testament—highlight Jesus's life and ministry on this earth. But Jesus does not enter the picture in the New Testament. The book of John points us to Jesus's harmonious relationship with God from the beginning of time. This brings us to a greater understanding of His divinity. Not only was He with God; He is God. He participated in the creation of the universe, and not one thing was created apart from Him.

As God the Son, Jesus is differentiated from God the Father and God the Spirit. Jesus is one with the Father and the Spirit in glory and substance, yet He is unique in nature. One way that Jesus, the Son, differentiates from the Father and the Spirit is that He is fully man and fully God. He came to live and walk among us in human form, learning, growing, and facing life as anyone would. John refers to Jesus as the Eternal Word, highlighting Jesus's role as One who comes in the flesh to reveal God to the world (John 1:1–18). He not only spoke the words of God; Jesus embodied all Scripture says about who God is.

How can Jesus be a man and also God? He has a real divine nature and a real human nature. God the Son put on flesh and became a man to reconcile us to God the Father through the power of God the Spirit. That is the wondrous work of the Trinity. When He became a man, Jesus "emptied himself " (Philippians 2:7). This does not mean He got rid of His divine nature. Instead, He willingly emptied Himself of certain divine privileges. As He set aside those privileges, He took on all essential human attributes, including basic human needs and weaknesses. This was made evident at His birth when He entered the world as a baby, needy and helpless. He relied on His mother, Mary, for nutrition and care. He was exposed to all of the natural elements of this world. He was raised as a child under His mother and earthly father's care. He worked and ate and slept. He grew and learned and took on humanity in full.

Both Jesus's divinity and humanity were necessary for our salvation. He needed to be perfectly man and perfectly God. Jesus's humanity was essential to take our place on the cross—to bear the wrath of God reserved for sinners because a perfect sacrifice was necessary. Tested in every way, Jesus lived a perfect and sinless life. As a baby, as a child, as a teenager, and as an adult, He never sinned. He never disobeyed His parents, succumbed to peer pressure, lusted or coveted, or gave into greedy or selfish desires. He was perfectly righteous. Every moment He was given the opportunity to indulge in sin, He did not. Satan even met Him in the wilderness to tempt Him even more, but Jesus never gave in. He knew grief, pain, family, friendship, joy, and sadness—He even knew death. Anything we know, feel, or experience, Jesus sympathizes with and understands completely (Hebrews 4:15).

Jesus needed to live, die, and rise from the grave in order to obey the perfect will of the Father. He needed to be divine to bear the full weight of God's wrath on the cross and satisfy the payment necessary for sin. No true human could bear God's wrath unto death and rise from the grave three days later. Only the divine Son of God could be the perfect sacrifice, rise from the grave, and seat Himself at the right hand of the Father in heaven. By His perfect life and perfect death, Jesus pays the penalty for our sin in full, restoring our relationship with God. By His resurrection, He secures that relationship once and for all, forever.

Jesus had to be perfectly human in order to suffer from sin and death and sympathize with our weaknesses. And He had to be perfectly divine in order to satisfy God's wrath and secure our relationship with God. Jesus now sits enthroned in the heavens, advocating to the Father on behalf of all who put their faith in Him. He is the only way to God. John 14:6 records Jesus saying, "I am the way, the truth, and the life. No one comes to the Father except through me." Our sin creates a chasm between God and us. But Jesus bridges the gap.

Jesus is the solution to life's greatest problem: sin. He wipes our slate clean and holds no record against us. Jesus gives us a new heart to know, love, and enjoy God forever. And He is the fulfillment to our greatest longing: to be perfectly known yet still perfectly loved. Jesus knows the deepest and darkest parts of us. In fact, He died for us at our worst (Romans 5:8), yet His love is so powerful, so enduring, and so faithful, that He moved from heaven to earth in order to come near and save us. He is our only hope—Jesus, only Jesus.

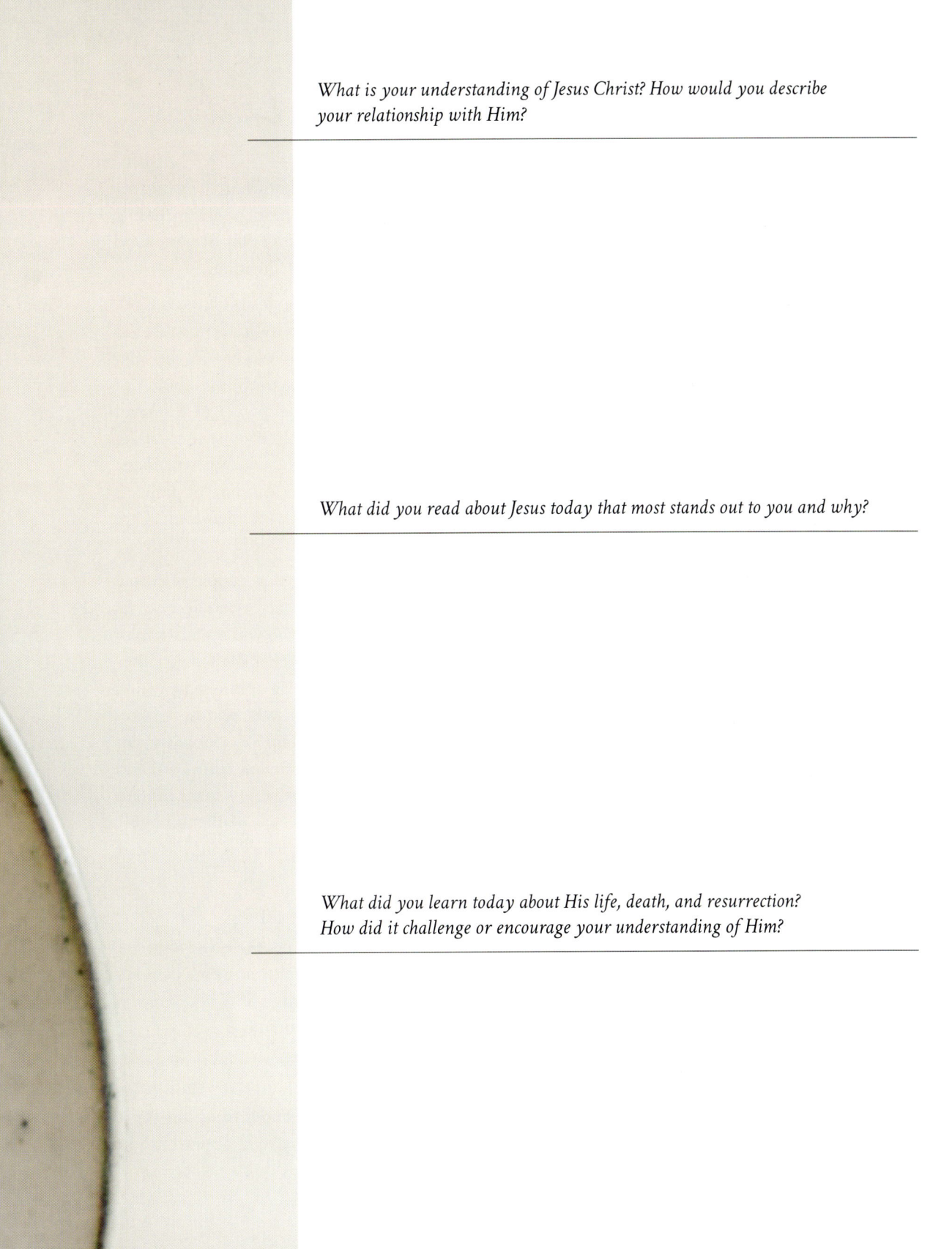

What is your understanding of Jesus Christ? How would you describe your relationship with Him?

What did you read about Jesus today that most stands out to you and why?

What did you learn today about His life, death, and resurrection? How did it challenge or encourage your understanding of Him?

C.S. Lewis: Liar, Lunatic, or Lord

C.S. Lewis is a well-known Christian apologist. He is perhaps most well known in the world for his children's book series, *The Chronicles of Narnia*. But he authored many more books, including *Mere Christianity*, which focuses on the fundamental truths of the Christian faith. Because God works in these wonderful ways, C.S. Lewis was an atheist turned devout Christian.

One thing C.S. Lewis explains well in his work is the essential truth that Jesus Christ is God. He uses evidence of the resurrection to point to the power and authority Jesus possesses as God. He succinctly explains an idea espoused by people such as Sir Thomas Moore in 1534, G. K. Chesterton in 1925, and Watchman Nee in 1936. The idea was that Jesus could not simply be a good moral human while also possessing the supernatural power to resurrect from the dead, and if He did not resurrect from the dead, how can He truly save us? Paul teaches in the New Testament, "And if Christ has not been raised, your faith is worthless; you are still in your sins" (1 Corinthians 15:17). Therefore, our understanding of Jesus as both human and divine is crucial to our belief in His resurrection. In *Mere Christianity*, C.S. Lewis expounds on this teaching:

> I am trying here to prevent anyone saying the really foolish thing that people often say about Him: "I'm ready to accept Jesus as a great moral teacher, but I don't accept His claim to be God." That is the one thing we must not say. A man who was merely a man and said the sort of things Jesus said would not be a great moral teacher. He would either be a lunatic—on the level with the man who says he is a poached egg—or else he would be the Devil of Hell. You must make your choice. Either this man was, and is, the Son of God: or else a madman or something worse. You can shut Him up for a fool, you can spit at Him and kill Him as a demon; or you can fall at His feet and call Him Lord and God, but let us not come with any patronizing nonsense about His being a great human teacher. He has not left that open to us. He did not intend to… He was neither a lunatic nor a fiend: and consequently, however strange or terrifying or unlikely it may seem, I have to accept the view that He was and is God.

He continues his argument a little more clearly:

> Jesus claimed to be God. His claim is either true or false. If it is true, then, *ipso facto*, He is God. If the claim is false, then either He said it knowing it was false, in which case He is a liar, or He said it not knowing it was false, in which case He was mad. Therefore, we are left with three logical options: He is either God, or a liar, or a lunatic.

In the New Testament Gospels, Jesus poses the question to His disciples, "who do you say that I am?" (Matthew 16:15). This is the question that we all need to answer: Who is Jesus? Is He a liar? A lunatic? Or Lord? Let us not shy away from this question or answer it half-heartedly. Take an intentional look at the person of Christ as you read about Him in the Bible. Your answer has the power to transform your life.

Who is Jesus? Use this space to journal through and record your findings as you investigate.

Scripture Referenced:

Verse	Takeaway

week 2 - day 2

"

The true, saving work of the gospel of Jesus Christ is a changed heart that results in a changed life.

There is Only One Way to Be Saved

READ ACTS 4:12, ROMANS 10:9–10, 2 CORINTHIANS 5:21

Many say all religion is man's way of figuring out how to get to God. Among other religions, this is said to be achieved through enlightenment or morality or achieving some sense of inner peace. These ideas center around the efforts of mankind and ultimately claim that anyone who works hard enough can access God. The flaw of this viewpoint is two-fold—first, it misunderstands God, and second, it misunderstands mankind. God is too holy to be reached by our own efforts, and He is too loving to leave us to our own failed attempts.

Christianity is different from any other religion in that it does not center around what we can do to get to God. Instead, the whole point of Christianity is that God made a way to get to us through salvation in His Son, Jesus Christ. God requires holiness, and we simply cannot attain it. So, Jesus attains holiness through His perfect life and offers it freely through the gift of salvation. Christianity is not works-based. It is not about keeping a "dos and don'ts" list. It is not about perfect morality or achieving enlightenment. Christianity is about the work of Christ in and through us—the work of Him living, dying, and resurrecting on our behalf.

God saves us not by our own righteousness—because we can never be righteous enough—but by the righteous works of Christ (Titus 3:4–5). According to the Bible, our righteous works are like "polluted garments" (Isaiah 64:6). Our best simply is not enough. We bring nothing to the table of salvation but our sin, yet Jesus takes our sin upon Himself and offers us His righteousness. What a grand and undeserving exchange! No one gets to God the Father except through Jesus Christ. Salvation is found in no one else—not in ourselves or our works, not in other moral advances, not in success or happiness; salvation is found in Jesus Christ alone.

God's saving work begins in the heart. Because of our sin, we are spiritually dead (Ephesians 2:1). We do not simply need correction or change; we need resuscitation! When explaining salvation, people often present the analogy that we are drowning in the ocean, and we need Jesus to throw us a lifesaver. But in reality, we have flatlined. We need Jesus to throw us in the life raft and revive our hearts.

True salvation is understanding in our hearts who God is, who we are, and what is required to restore our relationship with Him. It is a foundational belief in the gospel of Jesus Christ. When we understand the holiness and worthiness of God, we realize our shortcomings and sin against Him. We see clearly the depth of our sin nature, and we understand our great need for a Savior.

Yet sometimes it is so much more than understanding who God is. The truth is that we can only have a human understanding of God—because of human limitations, we cannot fully understand God. That is where faith comes in. And faith is beyond understanding—yet it is rooted in some fundamental knowledge that we experience in our mind, body, and soul. Therefore, we can trust in the saving power of the gospel as the solution to our sin problem.

Repentance is also needed for salvation. Repentance is turning away from our sin, turning away from our selfish desires, and turning toward the ways of God. We repent by acknowledging our sin before a holy God—inwardly, by believing it in our hearts, and outwardly, through verbal confession to God. When we repent, we lay down our lives in humility and gratitude in order to follow Jesus Christ. We look to the Bible to see how to walk in love and obedience. Repentance goes hand in hand with salvation. Our salvation in Jesus Christ is a catalyst for our repentance of sin, and our repentance is evidence of our salvation in Christ. We can turn from ourselves and our sin because we believe Jesus Christ can actually save us from it. We can place our ultimate hope and trust in Him to bring us spiritual and eternal life.

We may think we can pray a simple prayer or make a confession, and then instantly, everything will change. But the true, saving work of the gospel of Jesus Christ is a changed heart that results in a changed life. Our works cannot save us, but true salvation will be the fruit of God's good work in us. This change does not happen overnight, but it is refined over time and seasons and circumstances. James 1:3 says that the testing of our faith produces endurance, which can also be translated as "steadfastness." Faith in Jesus Christ that remains steadfast throughout our greatest joys and hardships in this life reveals the evidence of true salvation. And the beauty and comfort of our faith is the fact that God will help us all the way through until He takes us home to heaven. In the same way that God saves us through Christ, God also sustains us through Christ. And when the end of this life comes, God will make us complete in Christ.

"Salvation is found in Jesus Christ alone."

What is your understanding of salvation? What people, things, or ideas have you relied on to save you?

What does the Bible say about salvation? What role do confession and repentance have in salvation?

How does the Bible communicate that Jesus is the only way to get to God? How does the work of Jesus compare to other religions or our own moral efforts?

Week 2 Day 2 / 45

week 2 - day 3

"

When we receive salvation, God looks at us the same way He looks at Christ.

New Identity

GALATIANS 2:20, 2 CORINTHIANS 5:17

We search for our identity in many things. Our identity is the core of who we are and what we live for. We may try to find our identity in a career, working for the next promotion or raise. We may try to find our identity in the various titles we hold or do not hold as a wife, mother, employee, friend, etc., not knowing what to do if any of those titles are lost or never attained. We may search for our identity in material wealth, assessing our worth by what we have. We might even find our identity in past experiences and hardships, unable to view our lives outside of the lens of those things.

The truth about identity is that we were created to find our identity in God. It is sometimes said that we were made with a God-sized hole in our hearts, and nothing else can fill it but Him. The core of who we are and what we live for is found in God alone. Ephesians 2:10 says, "For we are his workmanship, created in Christ Jesus for good works, which God prepared ahead of time for us to do." This means that there are specific things that God prepared for us to do, and we can only discover that if our identity is rooted in Him.

Sin distorts the way we search for our identity and leaves us lost and without true purpose. But through Jesus Christ, God gives us a new identity in Him. He reminds us of who we really are—His—and what we were really made for—to live with Him. When we receive salvation, God looks at us the same way He looks at Christ. Our sins no longer mar our image, but we rest in the reflection of Christ's righteousness as God's people, dearly loved.

In Christ, we gain access to God as His children. We are adopted as sons and daughters, and we possess the title of heirs of Christ. We can approach God as representatives of His family. We can call a holy God our Father. What a gift to know Him in such a relational and familial way! Jesus Christ made a way for us to enter into the family of God, no longer orphans or strangers, but as near as a child is to their father. It is only through salvation that we are offered a relationship with God in such a personal way (John 14:6).

We find a new life in Jesus Christ. Our former ways, our sins, and our shortcomings no longer determine the trajectory of our lives. We once were destined to be recipients of God's wrath, but because of Jesus, we are given true and lasting purpose and identity in His Son. New life in Christ through the gift of salvation is the greatest news the world will ever hear. We are not only spared from death, but we are given something in which we can hope. Better yet, we are given Someone in whom we can hope. Our destiny, our purpose, our hope are secured in Jesus Christ.

Understanding life in Jesus Christ as new creations with new meaning and purpose can sometimes leave us with a fairytale view of the rest of our lives. The prosperity gospel is a false gospel that claims that if you are faithful to God, He will give you what you want. It preaches that life as a Christian should result in fortune and blessings, but that is just not true. Jesus says we will have trouble in this world (John 16:33). When we look around, evidence of brokenness is everywhere.

We see the reality of grief and pain, sickness and sorrow. We see cancer diagnoses, news headlines of heart-wrenching tragedies, death, division, and the list goes on. We are made new, but we are still surrounded by and tempted by sin. We will still wrestle with it and be affected by it. We still struggle with believing lies and trying to take matters into our own hands. We will have to fight against sin every single day.

It should not surprise us that the life of a Christian is not a life of ease, but the difference is that Christians have hope and help beyond this world. In this world, we will have trouble, but Jesus has overcome the world. There are greater things to come for God's people. The world is broken, and God is the only One who can truly redeem and restore it. This life does not compare to the beauty and fullness of eternity in God's kingdom. This life is just the beginning. When Christ returns, we will not simply be made new, embracing our identity in full, but we will also be made whole and complete.

> "Our destiny, our purpose, our hope are secured in Jesus Christ."

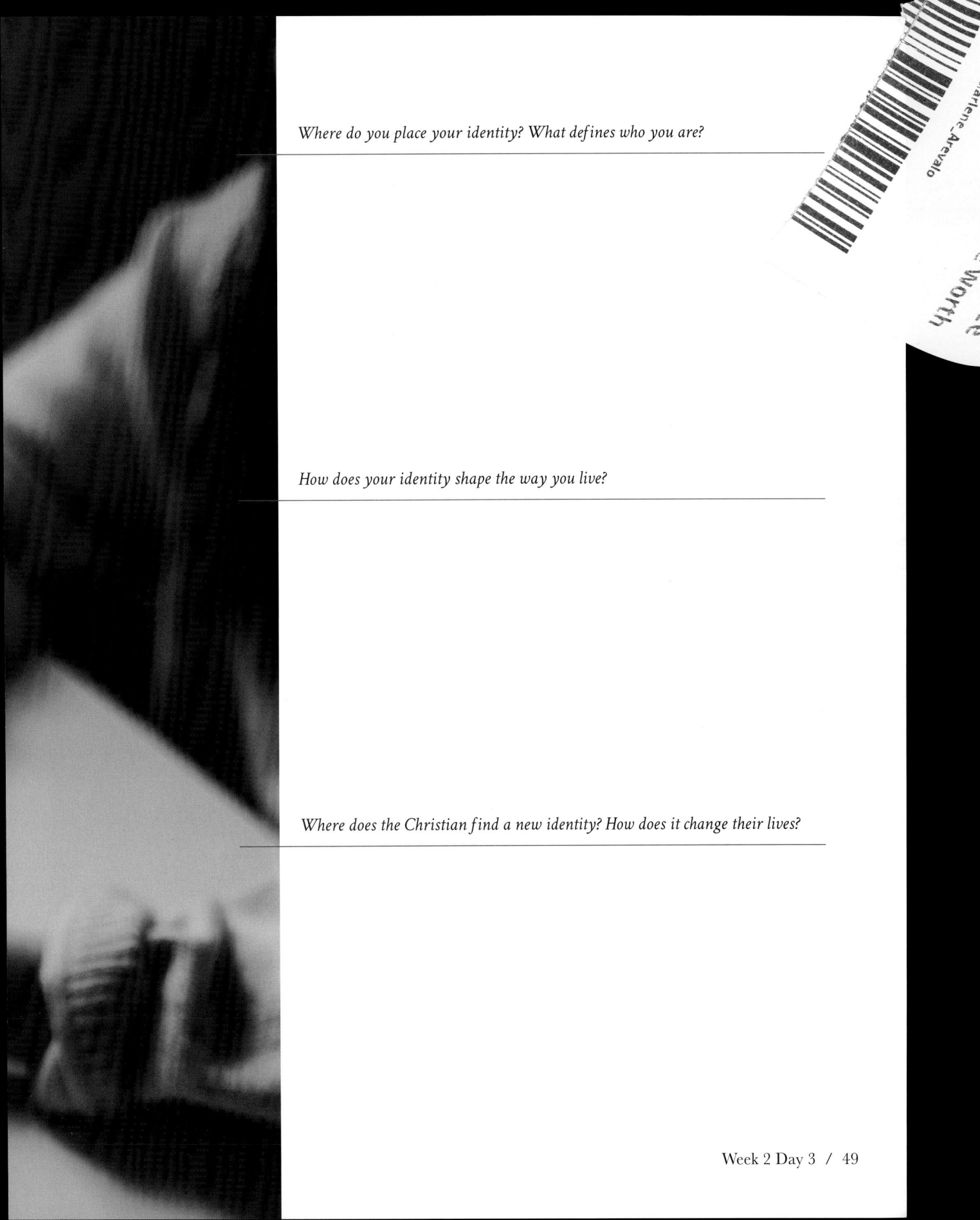

Where do you place your identity? What defines who you are?

How does your identity shape the way you live?

Where does the Christian find a new identity? How does it change their lives?

week 2 - day 4

"

The Holy Spirit is given as a gift to live inside those who put their hope and faith in Jesus.

The Holy Spirit

READ JOHN 14:17, EPHESIANS 1:13–14, 1 THESSALONIANS 5:23

When Jesus Christ saves, He seals. This means that He gifts us with the Holy Spirit. The Holy Spirit is one of the three persons of the Trinity. Just as the name entails, the Holy Spirit is the Spirit of God. The Holy Spirit possesses all of the divine attributes of God the Father and God the Son. The role of the Spirit is to testify to the truth of Jesus Christ (John 15:26). He unveils the truth of Christ in our hearts and makes known the truth of God's Word. Jesus explained the Holy Spirit to His disciples in this way: "But the Counselor, the Holy Spirit, whom the Father will send in my name, will teach you all things and remind you of everything I have told you" (John 14:26). The Holy Spirit is our Counselor and Teacher and is there to remind us of Christ's words.

The Holy Spirit enables and equips us to understand the Word of God. As 1 Corinthians 2:14 informs us, "the person without the Spirit does not receive what comes from God's Spirit, because it is foolishness to him; he is not able to understand it since it is evaluated spiritually." According to Ephesians 4:18–19, apart from salvation in Jesus Christ, our hearts are hardened and darkened, unable to understand the intentions and instructions of God. Our sin alienates us from the truth of God. We do not choose it, but instead, we run to the gratification of our selfish desires.

But, when we repent from our sin and put our hope and faith in Jesus, we are sealed with the Holy Spirit. This means that God authenticates His promise of full and final redemption to us by giving the Holy Spirit to dwell in us. In doing so, the Holy Spirit guides, shapes, and works to help us walk in faithfulness and to grow us in the likeness of Jesus in preparation for the fulfillment of that promise. The Spirit equips us to know and understand God's Word so that we may remember it and obey it.

The Holy Spirit helps us as we continue in a world still plagued by sin. As we learn more about God and the way He calls us to live, our lives will be transformed by those truths. That work of denying sin and growing in obedience to God's commands and purposes is called sanctification. We are daily sanctified as we plant the truth of God's Word in our hearts. Daily, the Holy Spirit better equips us to fight sin and walk in the ways of the Lord.

The Holy Spirit is given as a gift to live inside those who put their hope and faith in Jesus, as a way of producing the fruit of belief in the life of a Christian. The Holy Spirit produces the fruit of the Spirit, which is love, joy, peace, patience, kindness, goodness, faithfulness, gentleness, and self-control (Galatians 5:22–23). These characteristics are in opposition to the ways of our nature, our flesh, but as we walk in the ways of the Spirit, we will see fruit evidenced in our lives.

The Holy Spirit works in us what we cannot work in ourselves on our own. With the Spirit's help, we will grow in love, patience, and kindness toward one another. We will grow in gentleness and self-control when provoked by our circumstances. We will grow in faithfulness to the work to which we have been called. We will grow in generosity with what we have been given. We will grow in peace that surpasses all understanding. And we will grow in the overflowing joy that anchors our salvation.

Christians are instructed through God's Word to be filled with the Holy Spirit and walk in step with the Spirit. In doing so, we are empowered to walk in the ways of God and grow spiritually. The Spirit convicts us of sin, tugs on our hearts, and leads us to ask for forgiveness from God. The Spirit also helps us fight sin by reminding us of what God's Word says and helping our consciences be shaped by the truth. This is a daily work of denying our sinful inclinations and giving way to the Holy Spirit's perfect leading.

The Bible teaches that as the Holy Spirit transforms us, we will put to death our old ways and put on Christ. We will look more and more like Jesus every day that we put sin to death. We will be perfected over time, hating sin more and loving God more. The aim of sanctification is to be made complete on the day that Jesus Christ returns to take His people home. To be made complete means to lack nothing and to be a perfect reflection of the Son of God. This is the future reality that awaits Christ-followers indwelt with the Spirit of God.

> "The Holy Spirit helps us as we continue in a world still plagued by sin."

What is your understanding of the Holy Spirit?

How has today's reading helped or shaped your understanding of the Holy Spirit?

What role does the Holy Spirit have in the life of the Christian?

week 2 - day 5

"

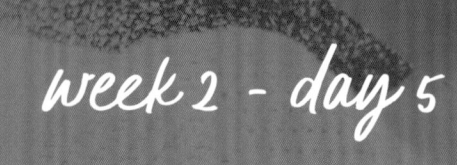

Jesus's second coming will bring God's story full circle.

What Happens in the End?

READ PHILIPPIANS 3:20 – 21, COLOSSIANS 3:4, 1 JOHN 3:2

When we talk about eternity and heaven, many may picture a bright white scene with glittering clouds and baby cherubs with wings and halos floating around and singing. This portrayal of heaven that is often plastered into books, television, and images is an incredibly false portrayal. Presented with this picture of heaven, many would say, *Well, that does not look very appealing to me, so I do not care to be there.* But the truth about heaven and eternity with God is that no image or description could ever truly describe it in full. However, the Bible gives us everything we need to know about what is awaiting us in the life to come.

For the Christian, eternal life is much more than entering heaven's gates; it is entering into the true presence of God. And when that time comes, God promises glorification. "Glorification" is a term that means we will be made glorious and complete in Jesus Christ. We will be without sin, and our hearts, minds, and bodies will be transformed into their most perfect state. No more sadness, no more sickness, no more bodily ailments, no more limitations, no more trials and hardship, and no more of the distortion and damage of sin.

This day is promised to come when Jesus Christ returns to the world to unite His people together under the banner of His name forever. The day that Christ returns is often referred to in Scripture as His second coming, and Jesus's second coming will bring God's story full circle. Everything in the Bible leads us there. Everything in life points to this moment.

But it will not be a glorious moment for everyone. There will be judgment, meaning an evaluation, and everyone will stand before the throne of God to give an account for their lives. For those who have put their faith and hope in Jesus Christ, their sins will be covered and accounted for. God will call them His people, and He will be their God. He will make a place for them in His eternal kingdom, and they will never know a day apart from His love and presence.

But those who deny Jesus and continue to live in sin will be held accountable. And the consequence of unpaid sin is death. This means that these people not only lacked the joy of a relationship with God on earth, but now, they will be cast from His presence forever into the kingdom of hell. Similarly, images of hell are often simply portrayed as a fiery dungeon of sorts, ruled by a red-horned devil, but the reality of hell is far worse than can ever truly be portrayed. Hell is complete and eternal separation from the blessing and presence of God. It is biblically described as a lake of fire, total darkness, where there is weeping and gnashing teeth. It is a place of extreme torment of the soul because God is not there. Apart from Him, hell is what remains.

God is where life and fullness are found. In eternal life and glory with Him, we will see all that He intended for us in creation. All of creation will be restored. The beauty we see now will pale in comparison to the beauty we see in the new heaven and new earth. What is revealed to us now we will see in full grandeur then. The beauty of the Venetian streets, the Irish countryside, the African sunsets, and the tropical forests will pale in comparison to the earth in its heavenly state. The sweetness of a strawberry, the smell of a peony, the softness of bread, the colors of the rainbow, and the delight of music will all fill our senses with joy in an uncontainable way.

The glorious promise of God is that, in the new heaven and new earth, all things will be made new! Jesus speaks of this renewal in Matthew 19:28, when He says, "Truly I tell you, in the renewal of all things, when the Son of Man sits on his glorious throne…" The restoration of the earth is mentioned again in Acts 3:21, which says, "Heaven must receive [Christ] until the time of the restoration of all things, which God spoke about through his holy prophets from the beginning." When that day comes, it will be grand and glorious. God will be there with all of His people, and everything will be as it should.

"The Bible gives us everything we need to know about what is awaiting us in the life to come."

What comes to mind when you think about the end of your life?

What is your understanding of heaven and hell? How does the Bible speak to these two places?

Everyone will stand before the throne of God to give an account for their lives. What might you say at that time? How do you think God would respond to your account?

Week 2 Scripture Memory

BUT THE COUNSELOR, THE HOLY SPIRIT, WHOM THE FATHER WILL SEND IN MY NAME, WILL TEACH YOU ALL THINGS AND REMIND YOU OF EVERYTHING I HAVE TOLD YOU.

JOHN 14:26

Scripture Memory Practice

Summarize the main points from this week's Scripture readings.

What did you observe from this week's passages about God and His character?

What do this week's passages reveal about the condition of mankind and yourself?

Week 2 Reflection

REVIEW ALL PASSAGES FROM THE WEEK

How do these passages point to the gospel?

How should you respond to these Scriptures? What specific action steps can you take this week to apply them in your life?

Write a prayer in response to your study of God's Word. Adore God for who He is, confess sins that He revealed in your own life, ask Him to empower you to walk in obedience, and pray for anyone who comes to mind as you study.

week 3 - day 1

"

His Word never changes, and it will stand the test of time and seasons.

Studying the Bible

READ PSALM 119:11, 18

———

We began this whole study by talking about the Bible. When people begin walking faithfully with God, the Bible is a lifeline. It is a bottomless treasure trove of knowledge and wisdom about who God is and how much He loves His people. It brings us comfort and help when life is hard and challenging, when we feel weak and weary, when we feel alone and confused, and in every moment in between. The Bible encourages us and strengthens our faith. It spurs us on toward greater dependence on God and greater obedience to His commands.

The Bible, however, is not simply a book we read one time. It is not introductory material to be flipped through and eventually cast aside. It is not a textbook or a novel but a window into the heart of God, and we will never stop learning about Him from its pages. Therefore, Christians study the Bible for the rest of their lives because they want to grow in their understanding and knowledge of God every day.

When we come to the saving knowledge of God through salvation in Jesus Christ, the Bible reminds us of our new identities in Him. It provides an anchor for our fleeting thoughts and ever-changing emotions. The Bible draws us back into the purpose and the mission God has for His people when we are tempted to go another way. His Word never changes, and it will stand the test of time and seasons. We no longer need to depend on relationships, wealth, recognition, or thrill to satisfy the longings of our souls. All of our hopes and needs are met in Jesus Christ. Even if He does not give us everything we want, we can trust that He does all things for our good, and the Bible reminds us of that truth (Romans 8:28).

The Bible provides us with wisdom for everyday life. Some may argue that the Bible is outdated and culturally irrelevant, but the Bible is relevant and necessary, not only for times long ago but for right now and forever. Though the context and culture may be different, the truths still apply today. The Bible may not tell us what career to pursue, who we should marry, or when to give our kids cell phones, but it does give us wisdom to help shape the way we live and make decisions. Learning biblical principles serves as a foundation for the way we view technology, the way we interact with others, the way we spend our money, and more. There is no circumstance we will face that God's Word cannot speak to in some way.

The Bible is for everyone, and you do not have to be a scholar or a theologian to study it. You do not need any extra fancy material—just time and God's Word in your hands. The Bible is accessible to every kind of person who opens its pages because God inspired it for the purpose of communicating Himself to anyone who reads it. There is no special formula for understanding it, just the Holy Spirit at work in our hearts to help us see the truth clearly.

Second Timothy 3:16–17 says, "All Scripture is inspired by God and is profitable for teaching, for rebuking, for correcting, for training in righteousness, so that the man of God may be complete, equipped for every good work." Paul reminds us in this New Testament passage that there is great value in the careful study of God's Word. The Bible is profitable for teaching us more about God and His purposes. It is profitable for rebuking us for the ways we disobey God. It is profitable for correcting us and pointing us away from sin and then training us in the righteousness offered through Jesus Christ. The hope as we study it is that we would grow into the person God designed us to be, shaped by His truth and delighting in His ways.

Like anything we want to know and understand well, we must study it. Studying the Bible can look a number of ways but most simply looks like picking up the Bible, reading it, and asking questions about what we have read. It looks like spending time with God by reading about Him. Some of the most helpful questions to consider as we read God's Word are: *What does this passage teach me about God? What does this passage teach me about mankind? What does this passage teach me about God's relationship with man? And how should what I have read change the way I live?*

The more we learn, the more we will grow in our love and understanding of God. In the same way that spouses cannot go through their days without ever talking and spending time together, we cannot simply go through our days without spending time with God by studying His Word in hopes of knowing Him and loving Him more.

"There is no circumstance we will face that God's Word cannot speak to in some way."

What is your experience with studying the Bible? What hindrances have kept you from it?

What value does God give to studying the Bible? How does it shape a Christian's life?

In what ways are you now encouraged or challenged to study the Bible?

Helpful Ways to Begin Studying the Bible

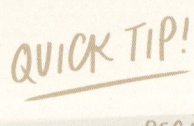

QUICK TIP!

BEGIN WITH THE GOSPELS

1. CHOOSE A BOOK OF THE BIBLE

The Bible is one big book with 66 smaller books. The best place to begin if you have never studied the Bible is in one of the Gospels: Matthew, Mark, Luke, or John. But every book of the Bible will be profitable to study.

FIND UNINTERRUPTED TIME

2. SET A TIME OF DAY

Whether first thing in the morning, right before you go to bed, or when you sit down on your lunch break, whenever you have uninterrupted time, utilize it to study the Bible.

PRAY + USE A STUDY METHOD

3. BEGIN WITH PRAYER

Ask the Holy Spirit to open your eyes and help you understand the text. Choose a Bible study method that helps you accurately understand the passage, both in its original meaning and in its application.

LEARN ABOUT THE BOOK FIRST

4. BACKGROUND INFORMATION

Before studying any book of the Bible, it is worthwhile to read background information in order to understand the historical context in which the book was written. One good place to find this information is in the introduction to each book of the Bible that is included in any study Bible. In your reading, try to answer the following five questions:

- ☐ *Who is the author?*
- ☐ *Who is the audience?*
- ☐ *When was it written?*
- ☐ *What is the purpose of the book?*
- ☐ *What is the genre?*

5. STUDY WHOLE PASSAGES

Read through the whole book of the Bible in one or two sittings. This can be helpful to understand the major themes in the book and how different parts of the book fit together.

READ THROUGH THE WHOLE BOOK

6. STUDY TWO TO THREE VERSES AT A TIME

Choose a few verses, and follow them in order from day to day. It is most helpful to break down the text into smaller chunks in order to get the most information. The Bible is full of knowledge and wisdom, and it can be helpful to study small passages to glean as much information as possible from it.

THEN BREAK UP THE TEXT INTO SMALL PASSAGES

7. OBSERVE, INTERPRET, AND APPLY

One helpful way to study the verses is called the "inductive method." The inductive method includes three primary components: observation, interpretation, and application. By studying Scripture in this order, we are able to better understand what the verses mean in context, and more carefully apply them to our lives.

UNDERSTAND THE VERSE IN CONTEXT

During the observation portion, we begin with the question: "What does the passage say?" To start, read the passage in context from start to finish. Many books of the Bible were intended to be read as a whole, and, as previously mentioned, reading passages in context can help us better understand the book's original meaning. Reread the passage multiple times, and note any key words, repeated phrases, important transition words, lists, comparisons, contrasts, etc.

"WHAT DOES THE PASSAGE SAY?"

Next, we begin to interpret Scripture, asking the question, "What does the passage mean?" In this phase, it is important to understand what the passage meant to its original audience before we apply it to our own lives. We can interpret the passage by looking at cross-references, summarizing the passage, noticing themes, or looking at trustworthy commentaries.

"WHAT DOES THE PASSAGE MEAN?"

KEEP READING →

Week 3 Day 1 / 67

OBSERVE, INTERPRET, AND APPLY, CONT.

APPLY THE PASSAGE TO YOUR LIFE

Now that you have finished the important work of reading the passage in context and understanding its original meaning, we can begin to apply it to our everyday lives. If we skip the first two steps of comprehension and interpretation, we risk misinterpreting Scripture or taking verses out of context to suit our desires. In the application portion, we can ask questions like:

- ☐ *What does this passage teach me about God?*
- ☐ *What does this passage teach me about mankind?*
- ☐ *What does this passage teach me about God's relationship with man?*
- ☐ *How should what I have read change the way I live?*

8. CONCLUDE WITH PRAYER

PRAY!

Ask God to help you apply what you learned in His Word to your daily life.

My Bible study action steps:

"When people begin walking faithfully with God, the Bible is a lifeline. It is a bottomless treasure trove of knowledge and wisdom about who God is and how much He loves His people."

week 3 - day 2

"
We witness God at work in miraculous ways when we practice this important spiritual discipline.

Prayer

READ PHILIPPIANS 4:6, HEBREWS 4:16

Prayer is often misunderstood. For those unfamiliar with prayer, it can seem like a sort of last resort. When nothing else is working and we find ourselves in complete and total desperation, we may make a last-ditch effort to call on God in prayer. This response may arise when we receive troubling medical results, face a life-threatening illness, or experience a great tragedy. But even with a grand misunderstanding of prayer, these last-resort responses speak to man's pursuit of something greater than ourselves and ultimately our need for Someone greater than anything in this world.

Even for those familiar with prayer, praying may often feel like a guessing game or a fumbling of words. Maybe it makes you feel uncomfortable to pray, or maybe you simply do not know how to pray. But prayer is much simpler than we often make it out to be. Prayer is spiritual communion with God. Jesus gives us, as Christians, access to approach God the Father in prayer. Apart from salvation in Christ, we do not have a relationship with God, and therefore, we do not have access to commune with God in prayer. But Jesus made a way for us to have a shared interaction with God through prayer, in which we speak, He hears, and He responds in His own timing and way. We do not need lofty words or perfectly curated language. We do not need to shield our true feelings. We can speak openly and honestly at any time to the mighty, wonderful God of the universe, and He will listen. This is an unspeakable privilege.

Prayer is an overflow of our hearts. How we pray reveals our true thoughts and beliefs about God, and the way we approach God in prayer says a lot about who we actually think He is. If we are praying for God's help, we reveal an understanding of His power and authority in our lives. If we are repenting of sin to God in prayer, we recognize Him as the One who made a way for forgiveness and righteousness. If we approach Him with our burdens, we acknowledge His capability to carry the weight of them all. Everything we pray about speaks to our fundamental knowledge of God.

In the same way, our prayers speak to how we view ourselves and others. Prayer reveals how we view ourselves in relation to God. We reveal what we believe we are capable of when we neglect to pray for certain things. We share our desires and hopes and fears and doubts in our prayers. We learn a lot about ourselves and what we value most when we consider how we pray. Prayer exposes our hearts. We pray about the things that matter to us (Matthew 6:25–33, Matthew 22:37–40). We pray about the things we care about. Consider your most frequent prayer request and what that tells you about your priorities. Our lives of prayer speak more of our hearts than we may have ever realized.

Even if we do not exactly know what to pray, the Spirit will intercede on our behalf in prayer (Romans 8:26–27). There are many ways we can practice prayer in a way that postures our hearts in worship of God and helps us fight sin. Even if we find ourselves falling into sin, we can come before the Lord in prayerful repentance. We can ask for His forgiveness. We can beg Him to bring us a hatred for sin and a delight in righteousness. We can even name specific sins we fall victim to and ask God to eradicate them from our lives. What a gift of grace that a holy God, through the mediating work of Jesus Christ, hears the prayers of lowly sinners like us. And not only does He hear us, but He delights in hearing us, and He helps us in every moment of need.

Prayer is beyond having a conversation with God. Prayer is a sacred exchange with God enjoyed through a loving relationship with Him. Through prayer, we are able to draw near to God for help and comfort. We are able to call on Him at any time and in any place. Even when we do not know what to pray, we are empowered by the Holy Spirit to pray in the way that we need to.

Christians are not only privileged to pray; we are also commanded by God to pray. Prayer is an active work of adoring God, confessing to God, thanking God, and making requests to God. We are not only instructed to pray when problems arise or when we need God's help; we are instructed to praise God for His good gifts, ask for His wisdom and guidance, and thank Him for supplying our daily needs. The Bible is saturated with the power of prayer in the lives of Christians, and we witness God at work in miraculous ways when we practice this important spiritual discipline.

"Prayer is a sacred exchange with God enjoyed through a loving relationship with Him."

What is your experience in practicing prayer? What hindrances have kept you from praying?

Why is prayer important? What value does it have in the life of the Christian?

In what ways are you now encouraged or challenged to pray?

week 3 - day 3

"

Boldness and prayerful dependence on God hold more power than knowing all the answers.

Evangelism and Fellowship

READ MATTHEW 28:19–20, I THESSALONIANS 5:11, I JOHN 1:7

Every Christian received the truth of the gospel somehow. Maybe a family member gifted them a Bible to read. Maybe a fellow classmate shared the good news of Jesus with them. Maybe a friend invited them to church. Maybe a coworker shared their own personal story of coming to faith. Someone may have even shared the gospel with you and encouraged you to read this study!

So you may wonder, why do Christians do it? Why do they keep sharing about Jesus, even after they have come to saving faith in Him? This is an important aspect of the Christian faith. In fact, the last command Jesus gave to His disciples was to go out into the world and share the gospel with others. It is how others hear the good news and come to the saving knowledge of Jesus Christ themselves. The work of sharing the truth of the gospel is called evangelism, and it should be an outpouring of the same truth that has shaped and changed our own hearts. Evangelism is born out of the overwhelming joy of salvation and the desire for others to experience it, too.

Evangelism, or sharing the gospel, is not simply intended for certain people like missionaries and pastors; evangelism is for every Christian, whether seasoned in the faith or a brand-new believer. Sharing the gospel can be scary and intimidating. It can be overwhelming because we never feel like we have all the answers. But God equips us with His Word and His Spirit. The Word of God penetrates hearts, and the Spirit opens eyes to believe in the truth they have heard.

Boldness and prayerful dependence on God hold more power than knowing all the answers. Christians evangelize with an ultimate trust in the Spirit to change hearts—no matter what the outcome may be—and an ultimate desire to witness the gospel at work in the life of another, to make the gospel known to every nation. Through evangelism, Christians offer others an invitation into God's family by sharing the story of Christ and the hope He brings. Who would turn down the opportunity to share the hope that can bring someone from death to life? All of God's people rejoice when even one soul is saved from eternal death.

New Christians enter in the family of God and enjoy a newfound fellowship among like-minded people. If you are familiar with Christianity or if you have been around other Christians, you have probably heard the word "fellowship" used. For those unfamiliar with Christianity, fellowship might be associated with a type of scholarship focused on people pursuing graduate degrees—but that is not how the Bible uses the term. Early Christians paved the way for this important practice. The term "fellowship" as used in the New Testament comes from the Greek word *koinōnia*, which communicates the idea of being together for mutual benefit. Fellowship is a means of Christians meeting together in a way that encourages one another and glorifies God.

Hebrews 10:24–25 affirms this idea of fellowship: "And let us consider one another in order to provoke love and good works, not neglecting to gather together, as some are in the habit of doing, but encouraging each other, and all the more as you see the day approaching." Fellowship is important because it is an expression of love and encouragement toward good works. Additionally, fellowship among Christians reflects Jesus to a watching world (John 13:35). The love Christians have for one another invites others into Christ's love. Christians are biblically encouraged to surround themselves with those who can help them along in the faith, and often this is best found in the local church, which we will expound on in the next study day.

The early church exemplified fellowship. The book of Acts tells us, "Every day they devoted themselves to meeting together in the temple, and broke bread from house to house. They ate their food with joyful and sincere hearts, praising God and enjoying the favor of all the people" (Acts 2:46–47a). Early Christians likely faced immense persecution with such counter-cultural religious beliefs. Even today, men and women all over the world face persecution in places where Christianity is highly disregarded and even banned. Fellowship together was and is that safe place, surrounded by people who worship the same God and live with the same mission in mind, where we can encourage one another to continue in the faith.

Christians need one another. We cannot walk through this life alone. In our fallen world, we will experience many difficulties and challenges, and we need help along the way. We need one another to point to the truth of God's Word, to pray together when times are hard, to help each other fight sin, to celebrate life's joys together, and to spur one another on in the faith. Christian evangelism and fellowship are God's gracious means of working through His people to carry on His message and to unite His people under the banner of His name. He will accomplish His good and glorious purposes. The question is, will you be a part of His wonderful work?

"Fellowship among Christians reflects Jesus to a watching world."

What is your experience with evangelism? Why is it important to the Christian faith?

What is your experience with fellowship? Why is it important to the Christian faith?

How does God use evangelism and fellowship to encourage and help His people?

week 3 - day 4

"

The local church is a beautiful gift that God has given to His people to equip and encourage one another in the faith.

The Church

READ ACTS 20:28, COLOSSIANS 3:16

New cultural movements and mantras suggest that you do not need to go to church to have a relationship with God. Yet, often, the generalized issues and criticisms people have regarding the Church come from a blatant misunderstanding of what the Church is and what purpose it should serve. Therefore, we will take an important look into what the Bible says about the Church and why a relationship with God and the Church go hand in hand.

First and foremost, the Church is God's idea. "Church" is drawn from the Greek term *ekklēsia* and is used in the New Testament to identify the community of Christians. It literally means "assembly" or "meeting." In the New Testament, Jesus declared, "… on this rock I will build my church, and the gates of Hades will not overpower it" (Matthew 16:18). From that moment on, the term "church" is exclusively used in the Bible to speak about the gathering together of God's people to worship and glorify God. It never has been biblically referred to as a building, a temple, or a house, but it has always referred to a people: God's people.

There are two ways that Christians today talk about the Church. The first is what is referred to as the local church, as defined by its geographical setting. If you notice, the New Testament churches were identified by their geographic location. For example, the church of Ephesus or the church of Thessalonica were churches composed of Christian residents in that city. The local church, when it functions as God designed, gathers every week to sit together under the preaching and teaching of God's Word, to sing and worship together, to connect with one another, to pray together, and to affirm one another in the faith.

The second way is referred to as the universal Church, which includes Christians from all times and places. The installment of the universal Church will happen when Jesus Christ returns and gathers every single Christian together under the banner of His name. This will be a glorious moment. All who have received Jesus Christ as their Lord and Savior will come together and praise God with one accord. What local churches see from a smaller expression, we will witness from the universal Church in a grand and tangible display. This is our entire family of the faith—the full family of God. And the nature of the local church prepares us for that day. God is committed to His Church, and He is committed to gathering all of His people together one day.

The local church is a beautiful gift that God has given to His people to equip and encourage one another in the faith. One of the central pursuits of the Church is to be a place where the whole body grows together into the likeness of Christ (Ephesians 4:15–16). There are many people and things who will try to replicate that—influencers on social media, friend groups, podcasts, virtual meetings, and more. But God gave His people the local church—a place where life happens around one another and people are actually known, encouraged, and held accountable for their actions.

The local church also provides a family. A family is usually composed of different ages, skills, careers, likes, and dislikes. It is diverse yet united. When a family functions as God designed, each member knows and understands one another, as well as how to help, how to spur one another on, and how to challenge one another when necessary. This close and intimate relationship cannot happen behind a screen or at a distance. Christians become one with the entire body of Christ, and every Christian serves an important role in the body. In 1 Corinthians 12, Paul explains that the body has many members, and each member has an important role. In fact, Paul says that God has put the body together (1 Corinthians 12:24). In the local church, Christians are to "have the same concern for each other. So if one member suffers, all the members suffer with it; if one member is honored, all the members rejoice with it" (1 Corinthians 12:25b–26). The local body is designed to be a place where you can forgive and be forgiven, love and be loved, encourage and be encouraged, challenge and be challenged.

Walking alongside other believers in the local church can be hard and messy. Sin and hurt will be sure to find a way in, as in any group or place on this earth. Do not let that be a deterrent from embracing the local church and becoming a part of the body of Christ. Allow these struggles to point you to the truth of the gospel and encourage you to find your ultimate hope in the redemption and restoration God promises to bring. As you walk together, the Church as a whole is called to prepare one another for the day when every local church will unite together as the one true Church under the banner of Jesus's name.

"God is committed to His Church."

What is your experience with church?

How does the Bible shape your understanding or view of the Church?

Why is the Church important for Christians? How does it affect their lives?

week 3 - day 5

"

God uses every opportunity to bring us to trust and put our faith in Him.

Reflect and Respond

—

As this study comes to a close, take a moment to reflect. Have your questions and curiosities about Christianity been addressed? Many may still remain, but it should be made clear that there is a reason you opened and read through this study. God uses every opportunity to bring us to trust and put our faith in Him. The truth of who God is and what He does for His people is astounding and life-changing and certainly worth considering. Wherever you are in your seeking and searching, the opportunity lay before you to reflect and respond to the truth about what you have read.

Romans 6:23 says, "For the wages of sin is death, but the gift of God is eternal life in Christ Jesus our Lord." We are all sinners, and the price we pay for our sin is eternal death and separation from God and all of His blessings, both now and forever. But this verse transitions with a very life-saving alternative, pointing us to the great and underserved gift God has given us. God offers us the free gift of salvation. He offers us the gift of eternal life, the chance to be united in a relationship with Him and His blessings forever.

But we cannot achieve salvation on our own. Our sin creates a chasm, an insurmountable separation, between us and our Holy God. We can choose to continue in a life of sin, ever trying to achieve our own standards of moralism or perfection. But truthfully, our efforts will never be enough. We cannot do anything in and of ourselves to remove our sin and restore our relationship with God. We cannot save ourselves. So how do we obtain that free gift? The gospel of Jesus Christ brings the good news of hope. Jesus bridges the divide. He takes our sins to the cross and makes a pathway for us to enjoy the presence and blessings of God forever. The key phrase to the passage of Romans 6:23 is "in Christ Jesus our Lord." It is only through Jesus that we find and receive the gift of salvation. Nothing and no one can offer us salvation but Jesus. He is the only One who can save us.

This is the gift that Jesus offers you through His life, death, and resurrection. To receive it, the Bible calls us to confess with our mouths that "Jesus is Lord" and believe in our hearts that God raised Him from the dead (Romans 10:9). This is a simple yet profoundly transformational response to the good news. And this is a response you can make right now—wherever you are and whatever you have been through.

This life is fleeting. We have no idea how much time we have left to live and breathe on this earth, and there is no way to be certain what the future holds. We would be wise to consider where this life will lead us and what will happen when it ends. We would be wise to consider who can truly save us. The truth is, there is only One who is righteous and mighty enough to save us, and He has invited us to find our salvation in Him. Eternity hangs in the balance, and Romans 10:13 reminds us, "For everyone who calls on the name of the Lord will be saved."

The gospel is too good to ignore. This good news demands a response—an active decision to turn away from sin and follow Christ. How will you choose to respond? Will you receive the invitation? Will you trust in Jesus Christ to save you from your sin? Will you repent of your ways and turn to walk in the ways of the Bible?

The story of the Bible is that every kind of person with every kind of story is invited through the work of the gospel to belong in God's family. This message is for you and will always be for you. The opportunity to join the Christian family and experience the incomparable joy of salvation in Jesus Christ is in front of you. The invitation is free, but it demands a response. Will you choose to receive the gift of life today and forevermore?

"Nothing and no one can offer us salvation but Jesus."

What is your initial response to the gospel?

Take a moment to list out your remaining thoughts, feelings, conclusions, and questions about Christianity as you finish this study.

Practice writing a prayer to God with total honesty and transparency. Ask Him to make Himself known to you through His Word, ask Him to bring clarity to your questions, and ask Him to change your life.

Week 3 Scripture Memory

AND LET US CONSIDER ONE ANOTHER IN ORDER TO PROVOKE LOVE AND GOOD WORKS, NOT NEGLECTING TO GATHER TOGETHER, AS SOME ARE IN THE HABIT OF DOING, BUT ENCOURAGING EACH OTHER, AND ALL THE MORE AS YOU SEE THE DAY APPROACHING.

HEBREWS 10:24-25

Scripture Memory Practice

Summarize the main points from this week's Scripture readings.

What did you observe from this week's passages about God and His character?

What do this week's passages reveal about the condition of mankind and yourself?

Week 3 Reflection

REVIEW ALL PASSAGES FROM THE WEEK

How do these passages point to the gospel?

How should you respond to these Scriptures? What specific action steps can you take this week to apply them in your life?

Write a prayer in response to your study of God's Word. Adore God for who He is, confess sins that He revealed in your own life, ask Him to empower you to walk in obedience, and pray for anyone who comes to mind as you study.

Suggested Next Steps

1. DISCUSS YOUR FINDINGS

Choose two to three questions that still remain in your journey to understanding God, the Bible, and Christianity. Consider a Christian you would be willing to discuss these questions with, and reach out to them to schedule a meeting. There is incredible importance in talking about our faith investigation with others.

If you have made the decision to put your faith and hope in Jesus and follow Him, praise God! That is our hope and prayer for every person who opens this study. We encourage you to share this news openly with others, especially those who have walked through this faith journey with you!

2. ATTEND A LOCAL CHURCH

If you struggle to find others to walk through this journey with you, the church is a great place to start. You do not have to be a Christian to attend church on Sunday. Find a Bible-believing church near you to start attending regularly. Speak with a pastor or staff member, introduce yourself, and share what brought you to the church. Often enough, faithfully sitting under the preaching and teaching of God's Word and gathering among other Christians can be a means by which God answers many of our questions.

3. OPEN YOUR BIBLE

There are many people with many opinions about what the Christian faith should look like, but the best place to search is in the pages of the Bible with words inspired by God Himself. Commit yourself to a book of the Bible. A great place to start would be in the book of Mark or any of the New Testament Gospels (Matthew, Mark, Luke, and John) to learn about the life, ministry, and teachings of Jesus Christ.

4. EXPLORE OTHER RESOURCES

If you wish to dive deeper into your study of the Bible and your understanding of Christianity, here are a few other suggestions from The Daily Grace Co. Shop:

Better Together is a discipleship resource intended to be used as a tool to help establish and guide a discipleship relationship between two individuals or in the context of a small group. It will guide you through the discipleship relationship and provide material for you to walk through together as you pursue spiritual maturity. This resource includes sections on how to articulate a testimony, how to share the gospel, how to study the Bible, how to memorize Scripture, and how to cultivate a life of prayer. The goal of discipleship is ultimately that Christians would utilize these types of relationships to flourish in the faith, love God more, and, in turn, seek to glorify Him with their lives.

Amen: From Eden to Eternity is a five-week study designed to teach the big-picture story of the Bible and show how every part of Scripture points to Jesus. The study walks through various genres of Scripture and helps show how everything—from the Law and the Prophets to the Gospels and Epistles—points to Jesus and His redemptive plan. The study gives an overview of the main points of the story and features daily and weekly questions perfect for individual or group study. Great for both new believers and those who have been Christians for years, it connects the dots between the Old and New Testaments and teaches why all of Scripture is important to every believer.

Attributes of God is a six-week study on God's character. God's attributes are His characteristics. They tell us who He is and what He is like. When we know God, we love Him, and He changes everything. This study walks through God's incommunicable attributes, which are characteristics that are only true of Him, as well as His communicable attributes, which are attributes that we are called to reflect.

40 Days with Jesus is a seven-week study that walks through the life of Jesus. From His birth and childhood to His ministry and teachings, each day walks through a passage in the gospels to grow our understanding of who Jesus is and what He has done. This study can be used as a Lenten companion, or it can stand alone. As you dive into this study, our hope is that you would learn more about the life and ministry of Jesus, grow in greater knowledge and understanding, and walk with Him for a lifetime.

Faith Questions: Truth Booklet is a guide for engaging conversations on the topic of truth. It assesses non-Christian worldviews and cultural movements that have shaped society's understanding of truth. This booklet offers insight into the revelation and authority of Scripture and explains why the resurrection of Jesus is proof of our faith.

Faith Questions: Suffering Booklet is a guide for engaging conversations on the topic of suffering. It assesses non-Christian worldviews on the nature of suffering and compares them to the Christian worldview. This booklet offers insight on the reason and resolution for suffering from a biblical perspective and shows how Christians can point to the gospel and the glory of God in the midst of life's sorrows.

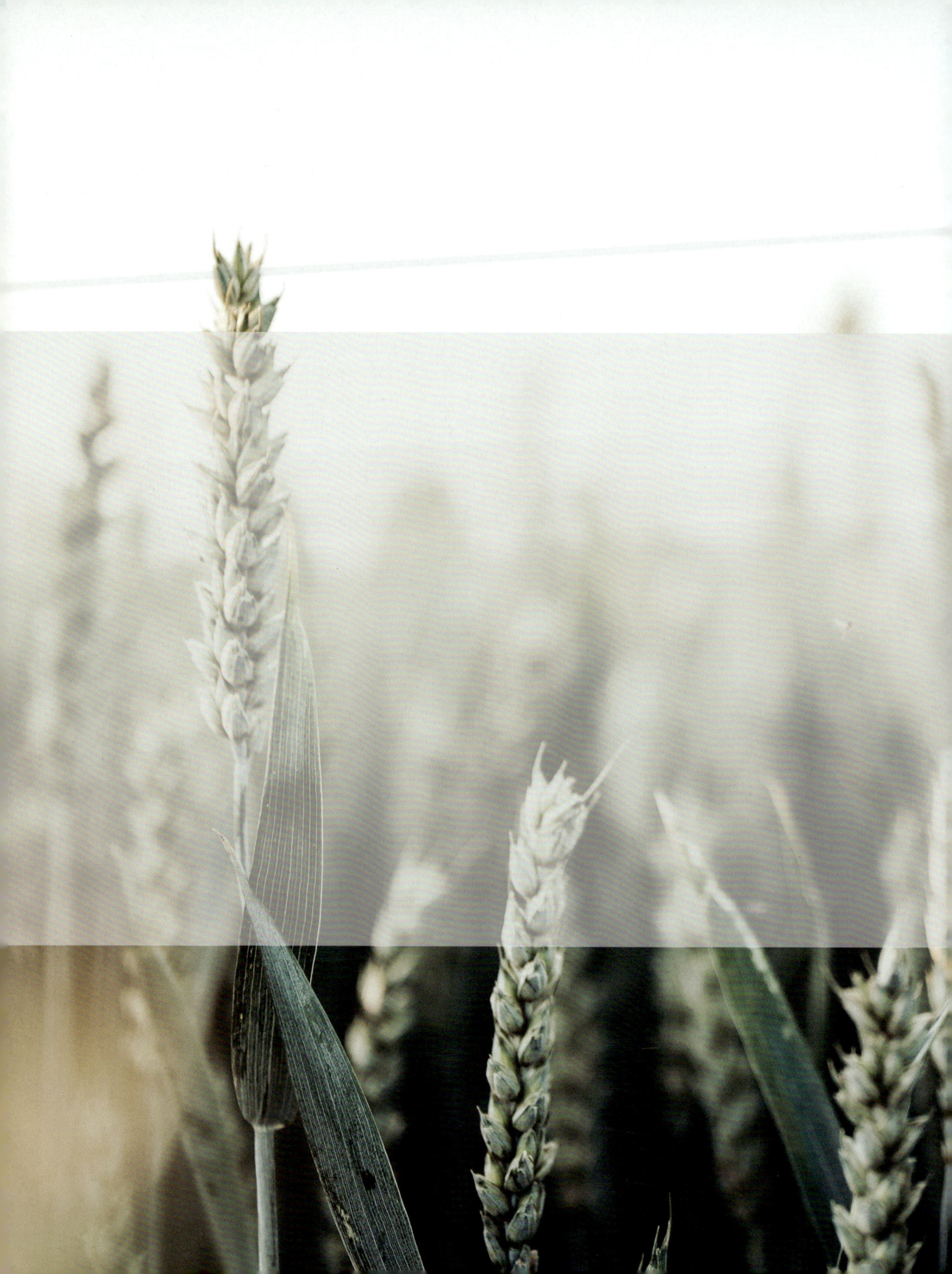

"The truth is, there is only One who is righteous and mighty enough to save us, and He has invited us to find our salvation in Him."

What is the Gospel?

THANK YOU FOR READING AND ENJOYING THIS STUDY WITH US! WE ARE ABUNDANTLY GRATEFUL FOR THE WORD OF GOD, THE INSTRUCTION WE GLEAN FROM IT, AND THE EVER-GROWING UNDERSTANDING IT PROVIDES FOR US OF GOD'S CHARACTER. WE ARE ALSO THANKFUL THAT SCRIPTURE CONTINUALLY POINTS TO ONE THING IN INNUMERABLE WAYS: THE GOSPEL.

We remember our brokenness when we read about the fall of Adam and Eve in the garden of Eden (Genesis 3), where sin entered into a perfect world and maimed it. We remember the necessity that something innocent must die to pay for our sin when we read about the atoning sacrifices in the Old Testament. We read that we have all sinned and fallen short of the glory of God (Romans 3:23) and that the penalty for our brokenness, the wages of our sin, is death (Romans 6:23). We all need grace and mercy, but most importantly, we all need a Savior.

We consider the goodness of God when we realize that He did not plan to leave us in this dire state. We see His promise to buy us back from the clutches of sin and death in Genesis 3:15. And we see that promise accomplished with Jesus Christ on the cross. Jesus Christ knew no sin yet became sin so that we might become righteous through His sacrifice (2 Corinthians 5:21). Jesus was tempted in every way that we are and lived sinlessly. He was reviled yet still yielded Himself for our sake, that we may have life abundant in Him. Jesus lived the perfect life that we could not live and died the death that we deserved.

The gospel is profound yet simple. There are many mysteries in it that we will never understand this side of heaven, but there is still overwhelming weight to its implications in this life. The gospel tells of our sinfulness and God's goodness and a gracious gift that compels a response. We are saved by grace through faith, which means that we rest with faith in the grace that Jesus Christ displayed on the cross (Ephesians 2:8-9). We cannot save ourselves from our brokenness or do any amount of good works to merit God's favor. Still, we can have faith that what Jesus accomplished in His death, burial, and resurrection was more than enough for our salvation and our eternal delight. When we accept God, we are commanded to die to ourselves and our sinful desires and live a life worthy of the calling we have received (Ephesians 4:1). The gospel compels us to be sanctified, and in so doing, we are conformed to the likeness of Christ Himself. This is hope. This is redemption. This is the gospel.

SCRIPTURES TO REFERENCE:

GENESIS 3:15	*I will put hostility between you and the woman, and between your offspring and her offspring. He will strike your head, and you will strike his heel.*
ROMANS 3:23	*For all have sinned and fall short of the glory of God.*
ROMANS 6:23	*For the wages of sin is death, but the gift of God is eternal life in Christ Jesus our Lord.*
2 CORINTHIANS 5:21	*He made the one who did not know sin to be sin for us, so that in him we might become the righteousness of God.*
EPHESIANS 2:8-9	*For you are saved by grace through faith, and this is not from yourselves; it is God's gift—not from works, so that no one can boast.*
EPHESIANS 4:1-3	*Therefore I, the prisoner in the Lord, urge you to walk worthy of the calling you have received, with all humility and gentleness, with patience, bearing with one another in love, making every effort to keep the unity of the Spirit through the bond of peace.*

*Thank you for studying
God's Word with us!*

CONNECT WITH US
@thedailygraceco
@dailygracepodcast

CONTACT US
info@thedailygraceco.com

SHARE
#thedailygraceco

VISIT US ONLINE
www.thedailygraceco.com

MORE DAILY GRACE

The Daily Grace App
Daily Grace Podcast